JUST WAR

JUST WAR

The Just War Tradition:
Ethics in Modern Warfare

CHARLES GUTHRIE
MICHAEL QUINLAN

Walker & Company
New York

Published by Walker Publishing Company, Inc., New York
Distributed to the trade by Holtzbrinck Publishers

All papers used by Walker & Company are natural,
recyclable products made from wood grown in well-managed
forests. The manufacturing processes conform to the
environmental regulations of the country of origin.

LIBRARY OF CONGRESS CATALOGING-IN-PUBLICATION DATA
HAS BEEN APPLIED FOR.

ISBN-10: 0-8027-1703-9
ISBN-13: 978-0-8027-1703-0

Visit Walker & Company's Web site at www.walkerbooks.com

First U.S. edition 2007

1 3 5 7 9 10 8 6 4 2

Typeset by Hewer Text UK Ltd, Edinburgh
Printed in Great Britain by St Edmundsbury Press,
Bury St Edmunds, Suffolk

CONTENTS

Acknowledgements   vii

I   Introduction   I

II   The Origin and Nature of the Tradition   5

III The Structure of the Tradition   11

IV   *Jus Ad Bellum*: Going to War   17
     Just Cause   17
     Sufficient and Proportionate Cause   20
     Right Intention   24
     Right Authority   26
     Reasonable Prospect of Success   31
     Last Resort   33

V   *Jus In Bello*: Waging War   35
     Discrimination   35
     Proportionality   39

VI   Conclusion   45

*Appendix A: The Ethics of War in Islam
             and Judaism*   47

Appendix B: Suggestions for Further Reading   51

Acknowledgements

We are indebted, for encouragement and advice, to General Sir Hugh Beach; the Rt Rev. Thomas Burns, Roman Catholic Bishop of the Forces; the Rt Rev. Lord Harries of Pentregarth, formerly Bishop of Oxford; the Rev. Fr Damian Howard, SJ, of Manresa House; the Rev. Fr Jack Mahoney, SJ, Emeritus Professor of Moral and Social Theology, King's College London; and Dr David Rodin of the Institute of Practical Ethics at Oxford University. Any shortcomings in the book, however, are entirely our own responsibility.

C. G.

M. Q.

I

INTRODUCTION

Moral accountability is a central part of what it means to be a human being. Every human activity must be open to moral examination, to questions about what it is right or wrong to do. That applies even – perhaps especially – to extreme activities like armed conflict, where some of the normal ethical rules, like not killing, have to be over-ridden. 'War is hell,' said General William Sherman during the American Civil War. It is inevitable that in war terrible things happen, things which in any other context would be utterly intolerable. But that cannot mean that anything goes. Almost every society known to history has had to face the reality of war, and has at the same time had some accompanying notion, however incomplete, crude or odd it may seem to modern eyes, of moral limitation applying to war – a recognition that even in the fierce struggle to prevail there are some things that absolutely ought not to be done, such as poisoning water supplies, cutting down the other side's olive trees (because they would take so long to grow again), executing disarmed prisoners, or killing women and children.

All the great religions of the world have contributed to this setting of limits, and so indeed have some non-religious approaches such as rationalist humanism. They have developed thinking on moral values, rules and understandings to govern and restrain the use of military force. Both the Islamic and the Judaic faiths, for example, have substantial concepts in this field (a brief note on them is given in Appendix A). The structure of ethical analysis that has been most widely written about and most extensively developed, however, is the one shaped over a long span of time by Christian thinkers in what is called the 'Just War' tradition (even though the historical record of Christians in observing it faithfully is far from un-blemished). Elements of this tradition underlie much of the international law of war accepted by all the member states of the United Nations.

For most of the second half of the twentieth century the countries of the developed world were largely insulated from the bitter experience of war by the paradoxically benign stalemate of the Cold War, under the fearful shadow of nuclear weapons. British, French and United States armed forces were often called into limited action, but few of these demands amounted to war in anything like the classical sense, and most other countries of the West had little or no occasion to use their forces in combat. Since the end of the Cold War in 1989, however, the realities of war have often forced themselves again more widely on the attention of governments and peoples. The United Kingdom and many of its allies and friends have had to commit their armed services to the use of force – with consequent cost in lives on both sides – in the liberation of Kuwait, in limiting murderous disputes amid the disintegration of Yugoslavia, in helping to cool brutal disorder in Africa, and most demandingly over several years in Iraq and Afghanistan. All these settings, in different ways, have served as reminders that moral discipline in the use of organised military power is still necessary and at the same time difficult – the more so alongside rapid advances in what technology can do and the frequent need for soldiers to use severe force in situations, such as counter-insurgency operations, which do not fit tidily into long-established classifications like formally recognised and declared war between sovereign states. (This book, however, does not attempt to deal either with situations in which the term 'war' is used metaphorically – as in 'the war on organised crime' – or with the use of coercion by the state in conflict-related tasks which may raise difficult moral questions but do not entail actual fighting, such as imprisonment, including that of prisoners of war, or interrogation.) Amid these changes the decisions which have to be taken by governments and armed forces at all levels have often become more complex and difficult, less clear-cut, leaving us in greater need than ever before of a workable and relevant moral compass.

In addition, the presence and immediacy of media reporting almost everywhere have brought the harsh facts of what armed conflict entails vividly to the awareness of publics most of whom have far less relevant experience and understanding of it than previous generations had. The need for moral guidelines that will be clear, practicable and credible both to the armed forces and to the peoples they represent and serve therefore remains as cogent as it has ever been.

In our judgement the Just War tradition – which has lasted and evolved through centuries of change in the forms of warfare and of international affairs – still provides the best available foundation for meeting this need. This book seeks accordingly:

- to outline the origin and nature of the tradition;

- to summarise the main features of its structure;

- to suggest ways in which it bears upon current problems, and a few respects in which it may need to be adapted or reinterpreted to remain a relevant and robust guide in the changing circumstances of the twenty-first century.

II

THE ORIGIN AND NATURE

OF THE TRADITION

The work of Christian thinkers in developing the idea of Just War did not rest on any particular interpretation of what had happened in biblical times, nor on appeal either to what is said in the Old and New Testaments or to ecclesiastical authority such as that of popes. The Scriptures revered by Christians do not give any unequivocal message about war. The Old Testament has a great deal of war in it without any suggestion that God fundamentally disapproves of seeing His people defend themselves by force of arms – sometimes indeed rather the contrary, and in ways that can seem uncomfortably rough to modern thinking. War obviously does not sit well with the spirit of the Sermon on the Mount, but the reported encounters of Jesus with members of the military profession do not convey any outright condemnation, even though they were soldiers of a foreign occupation. The thinking of Christian writers rests, just as that in several other traditions does, upon an endeavour, against the background of deep respect for the value of every human life, to arrive by careful thought at some rational discipline for an activity – war – which by its central nature must always threaten and take human life, not for the sake of killing but as an inescapable necessity to prevent or end harm.

Early Christian practices and outlooks on war were not systematic and codified, but many historians believe that they were predominantly pacifist – that is, that the faithful generally renounced war and condemned it outright. This would have been partly because Christians in those days, living within the Roman Empire, mostly felt themselves to be a separate and alienated minority; partly because the Roman authorities often persecuted them; and partly because military service required an oath of loyalty to an emperor who claimed to be divine. But all that certainly changed when Emperor Constantine came to power early in the fourth century, adopting Christianity himself and making it the official religion of the state. Christians had from then on to face up to and work out the tough and awkward practical responsibilities of running a state and protecting its citizens.

The pacifist strain of thought and witness did not entirely disappear – as the continuing example of the Society of Friends (the Quakers) in more recent times illustrates – but it was always thereafter, at most, a minority view. The great majority of Christians, over the centuries, have felt bound to recognise war as an unavoidable reality in human affairs, and to accept the necessity sometimes to take part in it. The task for moral thinkers and teachers on questions about war has then been to try to analyse and establish why and under what limiting conditions war might be regarded as tolerable. Many famous figures – Augustine of Hippo in the fifth century, Thomas Aquinas in the thirteenth, and others later – gave their minds to these problems. And the cumulative product of their work was what we now know as the Just War tradition.

Augustine, Aquinas and their successors did not shape their ideas only by abstract reflection without any actual context, as though they were in monastic cells. They recognised a massive practical problem which ordinary people, or those who carried public responsibilities, could not be asked simply to ignore. The reality that had to be faced was the pervasive fact of armed aggression and oppression in human affairs – the onset (for example) of Attila and his Huns invading Europe from the East in the fifth century, or the Moors spreading Islam by the sword through the Mediterranean and up across Spain into France in the seventh and eighth centuries. It was no good saying that in a well-ordered world Attila ought not to exist, or that if someone or other had done something different or wiser some time ago he would not have got here. The fact was that he was here, and Christians had to decide what to do about him. And the Just War theorists believed that it simply could not be right to lay down, as an absolute moral rule, that armed resistance to Attila or his like was forbidden. Given this, what they then sought to do was to formulate ways of bringing an ultimate right of effective armed resistance under the best moral

discipline – the most rational, the most consistent with
basic principles of natural law – that careful and prudent
thought could devise, without limiting that ultimate right
of resistance so severely as to make it useless in practical
terms.

That, in essence, is how we have got to the Just War
tradition as it exists today. It is important to note that it is a
very different matter from 'holy war', a concept which
from time to time has encouraged religious believers to
take up arms aggressively in the service, as they saw it, of
their faith. In historical practice that has almost always
proved pernicious, not least because it has usually meant
demonising the other side. The central thrust of the Just
War tradition, by contrast, is to control and limit war,
sometimes even to forbid it, and always to remember the
adversary's humanity.

The Just War tradition is sometimes described as a
'doctrine'. That is not an ideal term, since it may carry
overtones of something handed down from on high, or
fixed. The tradition is not like that. It is naturally indebted
to great thinkers from the past, but it is a living and
evolving body of thought, undergoing modification and
enriched by addition as understanding widens under the
impact of changing circumstances, the challenge of debate, and collective learning from varied new experience.

The nature of the tradition – open, and based upon
practical reason and humanity-wide values, not scriptural
or institutional authority – means that it is in no way an

exclusively Christian spiritual or intellectual property which others cannot adopt and apply. Nothing in it need be alien or repugnant to Muslims or Jews or those of other faiths, nor indeed to non-believers in religion who accept the special status of individual human life. This came close to being recognised, though understandably without explicit acknowledgement, in the December 2004 report of the diversely composed High-Level Panel set up by United Nations Secretary-General Kofi Annan to review threats, challenges and change in world security. The guidelines put forward by the panel to govern legitimate recourse to force closely paralleled the content of the Just War tradition.

III

THE STRUCTURE
OF THE TRADITION

The structure of the tradition starts from recognition that killing or injuring other people is prima facie gravely wrong, and that war is therefore in itself a great evil. As the United States General Bernard Rogers, NATO's Supreme Allied Commander in Europe in the 1980s, said in a debate in Oxford, 'Anyone who has ever been in combat knows that war is a bad and a stupid way of doing business.' But the tradition recognises also that, while war can never be positively good, it is not always the worst thing; there may sometimes be duties and responsibilities so necessary to fulfil, happenings so important to end or prevent, such as aggression against us or innocent third parties, that a general presumption against killing cannot be absolute for all times and circumstances. The tradition then sets out a range of tests – criteria – that must be satisfied if war is to be morally justified. These criteria fall into two groups: 'the right to fight', and 'how to fight right'. The first group, often referred to collectively under the Latin phrase *jus ad bellum*, concerns the morality of going to war at all. The second group, referred to as *jus in bello*, concerns the morality of what is done within war – how it is to be waged.

There are six criteria under *jus ad bellum* (and it is important to note that they all have to be satisfied; four out of six, for example, does not amount to an overall pass mark):

Just Cause We must have a proper reason for going to war, such as protecting the innocent, restoring rights wrongfully denied, or re-establishing just order. Revenge, punishment for its own sake, or upholding a ruler's prestige will not do.

Proportionate Cause Besides being just, our cause must be weighty enough to warrant the massive step of engaging in war, with all its certain or likely evils. For example, it will not be justifiable to go to war simply because we believe, however validly, that another state has unfairly confiscated the property of one of our citizens, or insulted our flag or head of state. We must have a reasonable expectation that the outcome will entail enough good (over and above what might be achieved in any other way) to outweigh the inevitable pain and destruction of war.

Right Intention Our aim must be to create a better, more just and more lasting subsequent peace than there would have been had we not gone to

war. The extermination of a hated adversary nation,
for instance, cannot qualify.

Right Authority   The decision to go to war must be
made by someone with proper authority to undertake
so grave a step. Historically, this has usually meant the
ruler or government of a sovereign state, as opposed to
an internal warlord or faction. (There are separate and
difficult issues, which we do not seek to tackle here,
about whether, when and in what ways oppressed
peoples may legitimately resort to arms in internal
uprisings against gravely unjust governments.) In the
modern world new and complex questions arise
about how far and in what circumstances international authority may be required.

Reasonable Prospect of Success   We must see a
reasonable chance of succeeding in our just aim.
War does not come with certainties, but we must
not take up arms and sacrifice lives if, on honest
appraisal, the likely result is simply death and suffering without making things materially better than
they would otherwise have been.

Last Resort   We must not take up arms unless we
have tried, or have good grounds for ruling out as
likely to be ineffective, every other way of adequately securing our just aim.

There are two criteria under *jus in bello*:

Discrimination   This means that in our conduct of
the war we must not deliberately attack the innocent. In this formulation 'innocent' means (in line
with the Latin from which the word is derived) 'not
involved in harming us, or helping to harm us'. It
does not refer to personal moral culpability, though
it still leaves open difficult judgements about exactly
who is to be regarded as not involved, as non-
combatant. By 'deliberate attack' is meant attack
in which the harm to the innocent is the direct aim
of the attack, or essential to achieving its purpose.

Proportionality   This means that we must not take
action in which the incidental harm done is an
unreasonably heavy price to incur for the likely
military benefit. The harm needs to be weighed
particularly in relation to the lives and well-being of
innocent people, but it is not confined to them. The
lives of our own military personnel need to be
brought into account, and sometimes even those
of our adversary. The principle of not using more
force than is necessary always applies.

All this continues to be a highly apt and robust frame of
ethical reference. It is the best checklist there is of the

aspects that ought to be weighed. The circumstances in which the criteria have to be applied nowadays are often very unlike those of the tradition's early years, yet they have evolved considerably over the centuries and, as the rest of this book illustrates, there are no grounds for abandoning any of them as having become obsolete or irrelevant.

The essence of the doctrine, however, is disciplined pragmatism, and judgement does have to be used in the application of the criteria to specific situations; they are not tick-box tests that can be used simply or mechanically. Changes in conditions and settings stand to affect how they can be brought to bear. Today's world is different in important respects – political, social, technological – from that of even a century ago, let alone further back, and the criteria have to be pertinent and usable in situations that may not be neatly classifiable as wars in the standard historical sense. The following sections seek to explore the meanings and workings of the criteria a little further, and to suggest some of the ways in which it may be necessary to think afresh, or more clearly and precisely, about applying them to diverse sorts of armed conflict in the twenty-first century.

IV

JUS AD BELLUM: GOING TO WAR

Just Cause

There is no comprehensive and exact definition – or at least none that is generally accepted – of what can qualify as just cause for engaging in war. Some elements, however, are clear. A country's right to defend itself against aggression is the most obvious one, and it is specifically recognised in the United Nations Charter. International law and custom acknowledge also that this right includes coming to the defence of allies if they are attacked.

Other reasons that have at one time or another been widely accepted as constituting just cause include putting right grave wrongs. The coalition war approved by the United Nations and led by the United States in 1991 to reverse Saddam Hussein's 1990 seizure of Kuwait was a vivid example. Armed intervention to stop the suffering of peoples is more controversial, since it clashes with the principle – also recognised in the United Nations Charter – of non-interference in the internal affairs of sovereign states. The NATO action in Kosovo in 1998, however, was widely, albeit not universally; supported as being necessary. Many people argue also that there ought to have been international armed intervention to stop the appalling genocide in Rwanda in 1994, and more recently to relieve the suffering in Darfur. International law is still evolving in this field, and the subject – often referred to as 'responsibility to protect' – has been much debated in the United Nations, though so far with only limited progress made.

In earlier eras of the Just War tradition the punishment of wrongdoing was often cited as an appropriate just cause. It is very doubtful, however, whether in today's world such a basis for military action – which could too easily slide into revenge – remains a sound concept unless it has a genuine and substantial forward-looking value, such as maintaining the authority of United Nations Security Council resolutions or establishing deterrent warnings against any repetition or imitation of the offence.

One of the problems in applying the idea of just cause is that in most conflicts – especially modern ones, where even non-democratic rulers have to give persuasive reasons to their peoples – both sides claim to have justice on their side. In the 1990–1 Gulf conflict Saddam Hussein could claim, not entirely groundlessly, that he had significant economic grievances against Kuwait. That does not mean that the criterion of just cause is useless as a guide to morality, or that we have to concede moral equivalence to everyone. It does mean, however, that if we contemplate war we should make a serious effort to understand our adversary's claims, and should go ahead only if we truly judge that there is substantially more right on our side than on his.

And then there is the difficult matter of pre-emption: using force against an adversary in anticipatory self-defence, before he uses it against us. This means attacking someone who has not attacked us, but it would be unreasonable to hold that it can absolutely never be justified, especially if waiting to be hit is likely to leave us at a decisive military disadvantage. Most observers would now accept that Israel was entitled to use force pre-emptively in 1967 against Arab neighbours who did not accept her right to exist and were manifestly assembling forces around her borders. The case – which the United Nations Security Council accepted – for United States action in late 2001 to overthrow the Taleban regime in Afghanistan, which was sheltering the al-Qaeda perpetrators of the 11 September outrage, was primarily justifiable not as retaliation but as pre-emption in the face of an enemy plainly willing to commit further outrages if it could.

The murderous unpredictability of terrorists able and willing to kill suddenly on a large scale, perhaps with exceptionally destructive weapons, is a new factor that may influence judgements about whether to use pre-emptive force against states aiding or harbouring them. Nevertheless, the concept of justified pre-emption still needs to be handled very warily, just as it does in other aspects of life (the state cannot reasonably throw into prison individuals who merely seem potential wrong-doers). The concept may easily slide from genuinely pre-emptive action into a broader and more dubious concept of preventive action: assailing someone because we do not like the look of him, or because we fear that he might one day do harm to us. The tests need to include an honest weighing of whether the action we seek to forestall is in truth highly probable (not merely possible) and immi-nent, and of a kind and weight that would leave us crucially damaged. The hurdle of justification for pre-emption should continue to be set very high.

Sufficient and Proportionate Cause

Simply to have the balance of right clearly on our side is not on its own a good enough reason for taking up arms. War always does harm – it always kills people, and sets in train sequences of events that are hard to predict or control. Winston Churchill once wrote:

> *Never, never, never believe that any war will be smooth and easy, or that anyone who embarks on that strange voyage can measure the tides and hurricanes he will encounter.*

It follows that even if our cause is just we still have to consider most carefully and honestly whether the good we reasonably expect to achieve is large enough – and probable enough – to outweigh the inescapable harm in loss of lives, damage and disruption. The Soviet invasions to suppress freedom in Hungary in 1956 and Czechoslovakia in 1968 were gross breaches of international law and the United Nations Charter, but the likelihood of major East–West war if NATO intervened was justifiably seen as too high a price to pay for opposing them, even if (doubtfully) intervention could have been expected to succeed. And it is especially important to weigh fully the likely harm if, as has happened increasingly often in modern episodes, that harm will probably bear very heavily upon people who are not themselves taking part in the conflict.

Moreover, judging the expected benefit is not always a straightforward matter. Commentators sometimes write as though it involves comparing the situation before the war with the expected situation after it: 'Will we make matters better than they are now?' But that is not the right comparison. Britain was in most respects worse off in 1945 than it had been in 1939, but that does not mean that fighting the Second World War against Hitler was wrong or foolish. The proper comparison is between the future situation we expect to achieve if we take up arms and the future situation we expect if we do not. And we have to recognise, too, that the comparison is not always to be reckoned in terms only of lives lost and physical damage done. There may be other values also at stake, such as freedom and the rule of law.

There is a further point to be noted. The comparison should not be between taking up arms and doing nothing. It should be between taking up arms and doing the best we can by other means – diplomatic, economic, legal and the like. And we then have to ask ourselves, if we judge that taking up arms is indeed likely to yield significantly greater benefit in terms of our just cause, whether that margin of benefit is big enough to warrant incurring the risks and penalties of armed conflict – and not just the penalties to ourselves; there is a duty to weigh the costs to everyone. Was the recovery of the Falkland Islands in 1982 – the liberation of a small number of people in remote and largely barren islands from unwelcome rule imposed by force – worth the costs of all kinds? Most people in Britain would answer 'yes', largely because of the important non-material values that were at stake, such as respecting the wishes of the people of the islands and not letting aggression prosper. Was the upholding of Security Council resolutions banning Iraqi possession of weapons of mass destruction – the central justification given by Prime Minister Blair for British participation in the invasion of Iraq in 2003 – based on good enough evidence, crucial enough and worth the predictable loss of life and damage to ordered Iraqi society? Opinion on that is more divided.

The Iraq episode, whatever view one may take of its overall merits, illustrates another complexity about the comparison required by the 'sufficient and proportionate' criterion. This concerns comparative probability. One of the diverse justifications put forward, at least in the United States, was that Iraqi weapons of mass destruction might one day come into the hands of terrorists who might then succeed in using them to inflict terrible damage in the United States homeland. That possibility could not, on the basis of what was known before the event, be totally disproved, but it depended on a chain of hypotheses of which the combined probability could not have been regarded as very high. By contrast, the like-lihood that the invasion and its aftermath would lead to tens of thousands of deaths was always far greater. The reckoning of what is justifiably 'proportionate' has to take into account not only the gravity of the likely outcomes of alternative courses of action (war or not war), but also their comparative probabilities. It is not legitimate to compare a worst-case view of one alternative with a best-case view of the other.

There underlies all the evaluations discussed above a difficulty that is uncomfortable but inescapable: they entail taking very serious decisions on the basis of esti-mates of complex futures, with wide margins of uncer-tainty and as a result much scope – often on both sides of a conflict – for different perceptions and judgements about where justice and prudence point. We ought always to have that in mind, and to try to maintain a degree of intellectual humility about our ability to foresee the future in matters as grave as war. But choice amid uncertainty is a constant issue in most fields of human activity, and it cannot be a valid reason for pacifism – for ruling out war altogether. In tense situations of actual or potential conflict, doing nothing, when we could have acted, is itself a choice, with its own responsibilities and problems of unsure prediction. Standing back from the 1994 Rwandan genocide, as the international community did, was not a morally neutral course.

Right Intention

The criterion of right intention means that our purpose in going to war must genuinely be to help create a better subsequent peace than there would otherwise have been. That plainly disqualifies revenge, or the annihilation of an enemy people, as legitimate aims.

In evaluating whether this criterion is satisfied it is important to distinguish between intentions and motives. In almost any complex human enterprise involving many people there will usually be a variety of motives at work, and some of them will be of a kind – personal prestige, for example, or domestic political advantage – the satisfying of which would rarely, if ever, be a good reason for the enterprise. That is inevitably true of war. Cynics or sceptics can often – and sometimes correctly – claim to perceive or suspect, within the mix that has influenced decision-makers, considerations which would not on their own be an acceptable basis for 'right intention', like reaping economic benefit or demonstrating technical prowess. That, however, does not necessarily invalidate the decision, provided the central purpose of the war is truly to achieve a better peace. Some historians have speculated that there were various ulterior motives behind the United States decision to use nuclear weapons against Japan in 1945, but there is no adequate ground for doubting that the central aim genuinely was to end the war as quickly as possible and with less further loss of life (on both sides) than if the weapons had not been used.

In the 1990–1 Gulf conflict critics suggested that the motivation of the United States and its partners was 'really about oil'. But even if the undesirability of leaving Saddam Hussein in control of massively increased oil reserves was (legitimately) in the minds of governments, the central purpose was to reverse the intolerable seizure of one United Nations member by another. That was an entirely adequate and cogent reason. More recently there has been a great deal of hostile conjecture about motivations underlying the invasion of Iraq in 2003, but even if some of it hits the mark, that does not in itself prove that the central intention must have been unjust or inadequate.

The duty to aim at a better peace is not to be interpreted solely in terms of benefit to our own side, even though we have special responsibilities in that direction. 'Better' has also to mean 'more just', and justice requires that we seek results that will be fair overall – that is, taking into account the interests of others, not excluding those of the adversary's people (even if the adversary government itself is regarded as a 'rogue' regime). That obligation has become increasingly salient in recent conflicts, notably where – as has mostly been true of the West, centred upon the massive military power of the United States – the likelihood of actual military defeat is vanishingly low. And it is naturally still more salient if the war is not forced upon the decision-taker but is in at least some degree a voluntary undertaking.

Military victory, especially if it can virtually be counted on in advance and still more if arms have been taken up voluntarily, entails a grave duty also to recognise, plan for in good time and sustain responsibilities for what happens afterwards. The burden of such responsibilities can be very heavy, as has been evident in Kosovo, Afghanistan and Iraq – so heavy, indeed, that its magnitude, and whether there is willingness and ability to shoulder its costs and difficulties effectively, ought often in prudence to be counted as a significant factor to be weighed in deliberations on whether to go to war at all. Some commentators argue that this is now such an important field of obligation that it ought to be classified as a separate and major part of Just War thinking: a *jus post bellum*.

Right Authority

The criterion of 'right authority' was originally framed, in medieval times, in order to make clear that the grave step of having recourse to war could not properly be left to factions or warlords within the state. It had to be a matter for decision by the lawful sovereign – whether an individual monarch or a collective supreme council – since overarching responsibility for the well-being of the people rested on the sovereign's shoulders. For most of more recent centuries this concept seemed to pose few problems, since the world – or at least the Western world centred on or derived from Europe – was structured as a multiplicity of independent states, with no suggestion that any higher political or legal entity existed to compete with the governments of states as the legitimate source of decision-making about war.

There was, however, a crucial change after the Second World War (following halting and ultimately ineffective steps taken earlier, between the two wars, in the League of Nations). The 1945 Charter of the United Nations, to which every member country has signed up, lays down that countries have the right to take up arms in self-defence, but that external military action going beyond that must be taken only with the authorisation of the Security Council. In practice, however, this latter provision has never won the full and worldwide acceptance and observance that it calls for.

This damaging failure has been due not only to the bad behaviour of particular countries (though over the past sixty years there has been plenty of that), but also to the shortcomings of the Security Council system itself – shortcomings inherent in its present composition and in the power of veto which the five permanent members

hold. Any one of the five can block a resolution authorising the use of armed force, however wide the consensus,
however strong and urgent the arguments in its favour,
and however arbitrary or inappropriately motivated the
majority of the international community may think the
blocking to be. (There is provision for the General
Assembly itself to take decisions, but this is a cumbersome
procedure that has scarcely ever proved workable if the
major powers disagree.) In a very small but important
number of instances the effect or prospect of this exercise
of veto has been so plainly and seriously unacceptable that
key countries like the United States have justifiably
thought it right to act without prior Security Council
agreement.

In 1950 North Korea invaded South Korea with the
aim of unifying the whole of the Korean peninsula by
force under Communist rule. The great majority of
United Nations members regarded this action – compar-
able with Iraq's attempt to annex Kuwait forty years later
– as intolerable aggression. The Security Council did
authorise military action to repel the invasion, and the
three-year war against North Korea (and, latterly, the
People's Republic of China) was waged by a UN-
approved coalition. But the Security Council authorisation was achieved only by chance. Not only was China's
seat still formally held by the Taiwan-based non-
Communist regime, but the Soviet Union happened at
the time to be boycotting the Security Council for

reasons unrelated to the Korean crisis. Had the Soviet Union been present it would certainly have vetoed the resolution approving resistance, yet it would have been unconscionable to allow such a veto to give the North Korean aggression a free run.

The NATO action in Kosovo in 1999, to stop Slobodan Milosevic's brutal and often murderous action to expel the Albanian minority, was a similar though not identical instance. The objective was not to change a regime – that came afterwards, by the action of the Serbian people themselves – but to halt what the United Nations Secretary-General had already publicly described as a threat to international peace and security (those being key words in the United Nations Charter). The leading NATO countries reasonably judged, however, that a resolution authorising the use of force to stop the expulsions would almost certainly be vetoed by Russia or China or both, and that to try for a United Nations resolution and fail would be worse – in its effect on the perceived political legitimacy of action – than not trying at all.

Opinions differ sharply about whether the 2003 invasion of Iraq, conducted after the failure of an attempt to get explicit Security Council endorsement of military action and on the basis of appeal to earlier Security Council resolutions which only a minority of countries and international lawyers regarded as constituting adequate validation, had 'right authority'. But the

examples of Korea and Kosovo (and, many commentators would add, perhaps Darfur, where widespread
desires for more determined humanitarian intervention
were held back by a perceived likelihood of veto by
China) do show that a rigidly absolute insistence on
Security Council clearance can at present be incompa-
tible with a proper recognition of the world's practical –
and moral – realities.

That said, even if Security Council clearance beforehand is not regarded as utterly indispensable in every
possible case of intervention, it ought to be regarded as
very important in the interests of long-term international
order, and its absence should be seen as a serious, albeit
not always fatal, shortcoming in decisions about intervention in humanitarian or similar crises. Moreover, even
where – exceptionally – it is judged that action must not
be held hostage to possible veto in the Security Council, it
should not be supposed that the say-so of any powerful
nation may suffice instead. There ought to be at least a
strong consensus (as there was over the 1999 Kosovo
action) among the countries closest to the problem and
therefore most directly and heavily affected.

Beyond this, it seems very desirable that the member-
ship of the United Nations should make more headway
both in defining the conditions under which the external
use of force beyond the situation of self-defence can be
legitimate and in solving or easing the problems posed by
the combination of the Security Council's current com-

position and the operation of veto power. Efforts were made in these directions at the 2005 summit meeting of United Nations members following a report on the issues by the panel of experts appointed by the Secretary-General, but only limited advances were made on the first issue and none at all on the second.

One other aspect of 'right authority', not often noted, deserves mention. Particularly in democracies, it is surely very desirable that decisions by governments to use armed force externally in substantial ways should be taken only on the basis of thorough and accurate information made publicly available, candid and consistent explanation by government, and careful consideration fully involving parliaments in advice and decision. In July 2007 the British Government proposed entrenching this last feature more formally in constitutional practice.

Reasonable Prospect of Success

The 'success' criterion reflects the truth that, whatever may be thought of an individual's entitlement to hazard or lose his or her life ('death before dishonour', or the like), it cannot be right for a national leader, responsible for the good of all the people, to undertake – or prolong – armed conflict, with all the loss of life and other harm that entails, if there is no reasonable likelihood that this would achieve a better outcome for the people than would result from rejecting or ending combat and simply doing whatever is possible by other means.

The criterion is occasionally thought to require that the decision-maker believe, after proper consideration, that there is a good chance of victory. This is rather too narrow. It is entirely possible to envisage circumstances in which something other than victory, at least in the classical military sense, can legitimately be rated as success. Preventing an aggressor from getting what he wants, even if his forces are not militarily defeated, can be so counted. There may even, though more rarely, be situations in which military defeat can qualify as adequate success if the fact of substantial resistance leads to an outcome less harmful than would have resulted from immediate capitulation. In 1939–40 Finland resisted attack by the Soviet Union, and though the resistance was eventually (and entirely predictably) overcome, it is likely that the settlement imposed thereafter did less harm to Finland than uncontested conquest would have done.

It is sometimes suggested that, even in hopeless causes, armed resistance can be legitimate as an upholding of national or moral values. This perhaps cannot be ruled out totally, but it would need to be assessed warily and indeed sceptically, since in practice it could too easily shade into defending the pride or obstinacy of the ruler rather than the interests of the people. And the criterion of proportionality – was the demonstrative upholding worth massive loss of life? – would still apply.

Last Resort

The criterion of 'last resort' does not mean that war is not to be embarked upon until every other option has been tried out. It would be unreasonable to demand that every conceivable non-military instrument must have been exhaustively tested irrespective of practical judgement about whether it is likely to work. The United Nations coalition against Saddam Hussein in 1990–1, for example, could not be expected to spend six months on a trial to see whether dropping propaganda leaflets on Baghdad would persuade him to withdraw from Kuwait. 'Last' must mean 'least to be preferred'.

Moreover, though diplomacy or other non-military pressure must be given a fair chance, in conflict settings time is often by no means neutral. As it passes, military options with their consequences may change, becoming narrower, more difficult, more costly in several ways, or not available at all. The early application of force may do more good and less harm than delaying until the situation has grown worse and harder to put right – perhaps needing more force and entailing more loss of life – as happened in the mid-1990s during the painful breakup of Yugoslavia.

Such considerations had a double relevance in the 1991 Gulf setting. First, the longer the expulsion of Saddam Hussein's forces was deferred, the more harm he could continue to do in and to Kuwait. Second, large military forces cannot indefinitely be held inactive far from home in awkward conditions without some loss of morale, readiness, efficiency and sustainability. That had been a properly relevant factor in the 1982 Falklands conflict, with the tightly stretched British task force poised at sea far from any base and the harsh South Atlantic winter looming. In the Kuwait instance, once there had been, in autumn 1990, a major surge in United States military deployment in the theatre to a level that could not have been refreshed by periodic *roulement*, the clock was inevitably ticking. Such effects are not just a matter of military convenience; they can bear upon the success prospects and the costs of eventual combat, and they may often weigh more heavily on one side than on the other. They are therefore a legitimate element of Just War assessment. That said, there can be no automatic presumption. It is possible to resort to military force too soon as well as too late, and no formula can displace the need for honest practical judgement in the particular circumstances.

V

JUS IN BELLO: WAGING WAR

Discrimination

We noted earlier that the criterion of 'discrimination' contains two key concepts: 'innocence' and 'deliberate attack'. Both need careful thought.

The concept of 'innocents' as people who should not deliberately be attacked does not turn upon whether the individuals in question had any personal responsibility for the evils which our engaging in war is intended to terminate or rectify. The word 'innocent' in this usage refers to whether or not they are involved (their own willingness or reluctance is not relevant) in contributing to do us harm – whether, in a different terminology, they are or are not essentially non-combatants. It was legitimate, in the Gulf conflict in 1991, to target the reluctant Iraqi conscript soldiers facing the armies of the United Nations coalition, even though they were in no way to blame for Saddam Hussein's aggression against Kuwait. The relevant fact was that they were there to help do harm to the coalition forces.

There are awkward issues sometimes to be faced, however, about what counts as non-involvement and who can claim it. Government leaders such as, in 1991, Saddam Hussein himself and his ministers? Civilians providing logistical support to the armed forces? Workers in armaments factories? All these seem plainly 'involved'. The broadcasters putting out a hostile regime's propaganda? Perhaps not always quite so clear. The old lady knitting socks for her grandson serving in the front line? Surely not. Disarmed captives? Also certainly not. But many such questions may become even more debatable if, as now happens increasingly often, the situation is not a tidy one of state-versus-state war but of countering guerrilla-like or clandestine opponents.

It is impossible to set a tidy rule that will cover all the diverse possible settings of armed conflict, but an honest judgement has to be made about what, in the particular circumstances, constitutes significant involvement. General attack on the adversary's population, for example in the claimed hope of weakening national morale or fostering unrest, cannot easily be justified. In Britain increasing discomfort has been voiced in retrospect about whether the massive Second World War raids on German cities by Bomber Command were morally legitimate, especially in the later years when the war's final outcome was in little doubt, even though the courage of the aircrews – who suffered very heavy casualties – continues to be rightly honoured.

Attack on 'dual-use' facilities – infrastructure, such as power stations or bridges, serving both military and civilian users – can also call for difficult judgements. In the Gulf War in 1991 there was substantial bombing of such facilities, but that was justifiably seen by the United Nations coalition – at a time when the rapid collapse of Iraqi forces that eventually happened could not be foreseen or relied upon – as an important way of weakening those forces and so shortening the war and reducing its costs of all kinds to everyone. Some of the targeting of Serbia in the Kosovo-related air campaign of 1999 – an unusual operation, in that it sought to compel a tyrant to stop maltreating his own people, rather than to disable his forces – raises more complicated questions, since it seems to have been designed in part to put pressure on Slobodan Milosevic by making life uncomfortable for the population as a whole. Yet it was conducted in ways that sought so far as possible to avoid killing people, and in the absence of other options for pressure the alternative might well have had to be a ground invasion that would certainly have had higher costs in deaths and damage. Given that the Serbian population did collectively have some power to influence the Milosevic regime (and in the end remove it, as events showed), the action seemed defensible within the spirit of the Just War tradition, which has always embodied a pragmatic approach to feasible options and alternatives. Nevertheless, the issue was not easy, and those who believe in the continuing relevance of the tradition may need to reflect further on how the concept of discrimination in targeting should be applied when the main aim is not to inflict military defeat but to change a government's behaviour.

The second key concept in the criterion of discrimination is 'deliberate attack'. It is an inescapable fact that in virtually any armed conflict (though the 1982 Falklands War came close to being an exception) non-combatants get killed. That is a consideration that must always be weighed seriously, but it does not make going to war unacceptable. The same is true of particular operations. There is a crucial difference between foreseeing something and intending it. We may well foresee that a military operation is highly likely – perhaps even effectively certain – to entail the death of innocents, but that does not automatically make it immoral, subject to a number of key provisos.

Firstly and most importantly, the death of innocents must genuinely not be part of the real purpose of the operation, or positively necessary (as distinct from unavoidable) for the achievement of the legitimate military aim. It must truly be an unwelcome side-effect – 'collateral damage', though that often-used phrase has a cold air. We may know that an enemy military unit is holding a civilian hostage, and that successful attack on the unit is almost bound to kill the hostage, but the attack can still be justified. We are not morally obliged to accept the enemy's holding of innocent hostages as giving him immunity from attack. The second proviso is that we must do all that we reasonably can, consistently with not thwarting or gravely endangering the legitimate military purpose, to reduce the risk to non-combatants to a minimum.

Thirdly, the likely harm to non-combatants must not be out of proportion to the expected military benefit. That takes us to the second *jus in bello* criterion: proportionality.

There is, however, one other aspect that deserves mention before we come to that. This is the issue of retaliation. If our enemy attacks innocents on our side, or does something illegitimate in some other way – for example, by using internationally prohibited types of weapons – are we ourselves then released from our normal obligations in those respects? The answer is 'no', or at least 'not necessarily'. If the transgression is a serious breach of some specific agreement or positive international law, then it is reasonable that the transgressor should lose his right to be protected by that. But we ourselves are still bound, by the principles of basic moral conduct, to abide by the concepts of discrimination and proportionality: 'two wrongs do not make a right'. Non-combatants on the other side do not cease to be innocents if our own are unjustly attacked.

Proportionality

The criterion of proportionality has essentially the same structure *in bello* as that explained earlier under *ad bellum*.

We must not do things, however legitimate in themselves, if in our honest and considered opinion the good
they achieve is likely to be outweighed by the harm they
inflict on those who ought not to be harmed. It is entirely
legitimate to knock out an enemy tank, but if we know it
to be hidden somewhere within a large hospital complex
it is not permissible to flatten the whole complex in order
to be sure of destroying the tank. It is inevitably often
hard to determine the 'proportionality' of an operation
that we are contemplating, since this entails comparing
two aspects of its outcome neither of which can usually be
predicted exactly. The possible difficulty of the evaluation
does not mean, however, that it can ever be brushed aside
as unnecessary or irrelevant. That remains so even when,
as in tasks where military forces have to tackle armed
insurgents or terrorists, it is difficult to identify the
adversary or to assess the side-effects of attacking him
when he is deliberately hiding within an ordinary civilian
environment.

Settings like Iraq after the 2003 invasion or Afghanistan
after the overthrow of the Taleban regime sharply illus-
trate some of the problems. Modern weapon systems are
more effective than older ones in striking accurately and
decisively what they are aimed at. But there is still the
other half of the task – that is, aiming them at the right
thing when the targets carry no distinguishing marks or
uniforms, or are concealed among the general population
and may well not care about (or may even welcome, for

propaganda reasons) the risk that attack on them may kill innocents. There remains no escape, however, from the duty to make honest judgements about proportionality on the best information available, even where uncertainties in that information have to be factored into the judgement.

Especially acute problems may arise, in settings like Iraq, about striking the right balance between self-protection and the danger of harm to innocents. Provided that they genuinely use the minimum force required, armed forces have the right to defend themselves, both for their personal survival and so that they can carry out their mission. But that right cannot prevail absolutely and unconditionally over the rights of everyone else. Suppose a serviceman is manning a checkpoint in unsettled territory when an unidentified vehicle fails to respond promptly to an order to stop. Should he take it out as a possible suicide bomber, at the risk of finding out afterwards that he has killed a terrified and disoriented civilian family that did not understand his signal? There is, once more, no neat formula to give the answer. It has to depend on in-the-circumstances probabilities that cannot be precisely measured in advance, especially perhaps by a young soldier with ten seconds to decide at night or in poor visibility, and not from an armchair with the benefit of hindsight. The obligations of effective morality begin, of course, at an earlier stage: military authorities have a responsibility to provide appropriate organisation, weapons and training beforehand, and also a set of rules of engagement that will make practical sense in stressful situations. But on-the-spot judgement will remain necessary, and the judgement has to recognise that in difficult and uncertain environments risk and danger is not to be loaded entirely on to one side of the balance. To take out the unidentified vehicle if the chances of its carrying a suicide bomber are thought to be fifty-fifty is one thing; to do so if they seem like one in a thousand is another.

Similar considerations and complexities can arise in other settings. In the 1999 Kosovo campaign NATO did not lose a single serviceman in combat during two and a half months of air bombardment, and a few critics seemed to regard this as somehow unchivalrous. But war is not a game in which we ought to give the other side a sporting chance, and the rightness of a military action does not depend on how much danger the actor faces in carrying it out (just as the willingness of suicide bombers to give their own lives does not in any way make their murder of innocents legitimate). If a commander can so shape operations that no one on his own side is lost, it is not merely his right but his duty to do so. That said, it was proper to consider – and NATO commanders did consider – the balance between flying high enough to be out of reach of hostile defences and flying so high that the risk of misidentifying targets became severe.

A further factor in assessing proportionality has come increasingly to be recognised as highly important: the duty to think carefully about the effect of military operations on the subsequent maintenance of reasonable living conditions and order for the people of the country where the conflict happens. This is part of the *jus post bellum* duty mentioned earlier, to face up to responsibilities for what happens after military victory has been won. In modern circumstances those responsibilities need to be recognised and planned for as a major element in the entire business of war. They can mean that restraint and a sense of proportion should be exercised both in attacks – however legitimate their immediate military purpose – upon infrastructure that serves the general population as well as the regime's war-fighting capability, and in the use of weapons like cluster bombs or land-mines that may continue to pose difficult-to-control dangers to people after the fighting is over or may do serious environmental damage.

VI

CONCLUSION

What we have set out in this book is no more than a broad general survey of how the Just War tradition bears upon the morality of undertaking and conducting military operations in the twenty-first century. (We offer in Appendix B a few suggestions for further reading, for those who may wish to delve deeper.) There are important aspects which we have not attempted to discuss at all, such as the special and stretching ethical issues posed by the possession of nuclear weapons for deterrence. We believe that the Just War tradition has relevant things to say there, but to go into them adequately would need almost another book. We have also not sought to explore the relationship between the tradition and the international law of war. Broadly, however, the Just War approach must include a moral duty to observe the prohibitions, restrictions and obligations enshrined in that law, even where, if the law did not exist, the tradition might not itself have imposed them in absolute terms.

In brief, though, we regard the Just War tradition as still valid and valuable. It was not framed in the abstract. It represents a careful attempt, gradually and pragmatically developed over many centuries, to put some moral discipline, some humanity, into the business of armed conflict without imposing a straitjacket so rigid as completely to preclude effective action against grave wrong. As practical circumstances change, the nature of what constitutes effective action may change with them, and the detailed expression of the moral discipline may have to be adapted. Much of what is happening in the modern world reminds us of that.

The tradition does not yield a tidy and unambiguous answer to every question. It continually calls for judgements, often contestable in good faith, on matters lying well beyond the expertise of moral philosophers. It is, from one standpoint, simply a systematic reminder of moral questions which we ought to think about when we consider embarking upon armed conflict or when we engage in it. But it is surely beyond argument that some framework for the moral analysis of war is necessary. Those who would reject the Just War approach have to face and answer the question of what other ethical roadmap they would propose to put in its place.

THE ETHICS OF WAR
IN ISLAM AND JUDAISM

The structure and categories of Islamic thinking about ethics in public affairs are in some ways markedly different from those of Christianity, and its teaching about war cannot be tidily compared with the Just War tradition. There is accordingly no explicit or exhaustive set of principles analogous to the systematic framework of that tradition. Many of the concepts used in the tradition are however also to be found in one form or another (sometimes indeed earlier) in the sacred texts of Islam – the Koran itself and the Hadith, the recognised accounts of the Prophet Mohammed's words and deeds – as well as in the writings of recognised scholars interpreting those texts.

In Islam there is a central emphasis on the primacy of peace, especially peace within the worldwide Muslim community. The key concept of jihad, meaning 'effort' or 'striving', does not necessarily mean taking up arms, though it does not exclude that as a duty in the right circumstances. War is in itself an evil, but divine law regulates it rather than forbids it; it can be justified to prevent the triumph of greater evils. The writings express strict conditions similar to 'just cause': self-defence, the pre-emption of imminent attack, the defence of Muslims' right to believe, the defence of the oppressed. 'Reasonable prospect of success' is to be found, and so is the concept of 'last resort', in the obligation to try negotiation for resolving disputes before war is embarked upon. There is a recognition of 'proportionality' and of the rights of innocents not to be avoidably harmed.

There have been occasional voices in the Islamic world, particularly in modern times, whose claims about what justifies the use of violence and what methods are legitimate, for example relating to the death of non-combatants, are sharply at variance with the Just War tradition. Yet these voices are far from being the majority or the accepted norm within Islam.

The Jewish pattern of thinking about contemporary war has historically been less fully developed than either the Christian or the Islamic traditions. This largely reflects the fact that for nearly two thousand years Jews had no sovereign state of their own and therefore no direct occasion to form a practical operational ethic of war. Commentary upon war mostly related to how to understand what was said about past events in the recognised Scriptures. But recent writings, following the establishment of the state of Israel, acknowledge such concepts as discrimination and proportionality.

Even where particular criteria from the Just War tradition are not readily to be found in explicit expressions of the Islamic or Jewish outlooks upon war, there is no element of the criteria that need be repugnant to those outlooks.

SUGGESTIONS FOR FURTHER READING

There is a massive literature – historical and philosophical – about the themes touched upon in this book. The following are among the books that seem most readily suited to readers who are minded to explore the issues further but may not have the time or inclination to do so as extensively and deeply as full-time scholars do.

Coates, A. J., *The Ethics of War*, Manchester University Press, 1997

Haleem, Harfiyah Abdel, Oliver Ramsbotham, Saba Risaluddin and Brian Wicker (eds), *The Crescent and the Cross: Muslim and Christian Approaches to War and Peace*, Macmillan, 1998

O'Brien, William, *The Conduct of a Just and Limited War*, Praeger Publishers, 1981

Reed, Charles, and David Ryall (eds), *The Price of Peace: Just War in the Twenty-first Century*, Cambridge University Press, 2007

Reichberg, Gregory M., Henrik Syse and Endre Begby (eds), *The Ethics of War: Classic and Contemporary Readings*, Blackwell Publishing Ltd, 2006

Sorabji, Richard, and David Rodin (eds), *The Ethics of War: Shared Problems in Different Traditions*, Ashgate Publishing Ltd, 2006

Walzer, Michael, *Just and Unjust Wars*, Basic Books, 2000 (3rd edition)

A NOTE ON THE AUTHORS

General Lord Guthrie of Craigiebank, GCB LVO OBE, was commissioned in 1959 and served with the Welsh Guards and the Special Air Service. He was Commander of NATO's Northern Army Group 1992–3, Chief of the General Staff 1994–7, and Chief of the Defence Staff 1997–2001. He became a member of the House of Lords in 2001.

Sir Michael Quinlan, GCB, was a civil servant for thirty-eight years (1954–92), thirty of them in posts concerned with defence. He was Policy Director in the Ministry of Defence 1977–81 and Permanent Under-Secretary of State 1988–92. Since 2004 he has been a Consulting Senior Fellow at the International Institute for Strategic Studies.

A NOTE ON THE TYPE

The text of this book is set in Bembo. This type was first used in 1495 by the Venetian printer Aldus Manutius for Cardinal Bembo's *De Aetna*, and was cut for Manutius by Francesco Griffo. It was one of the types used by Claude Garamond (1480–1561) as a model for his Romain de l'Université, and so it was the forerunner of what became standard European type for the following two centuries. Its modern form follows the original types and was designed for Monotype in 1929.